IMAGES OF ENGLAND

PERSHORE
REVISITED

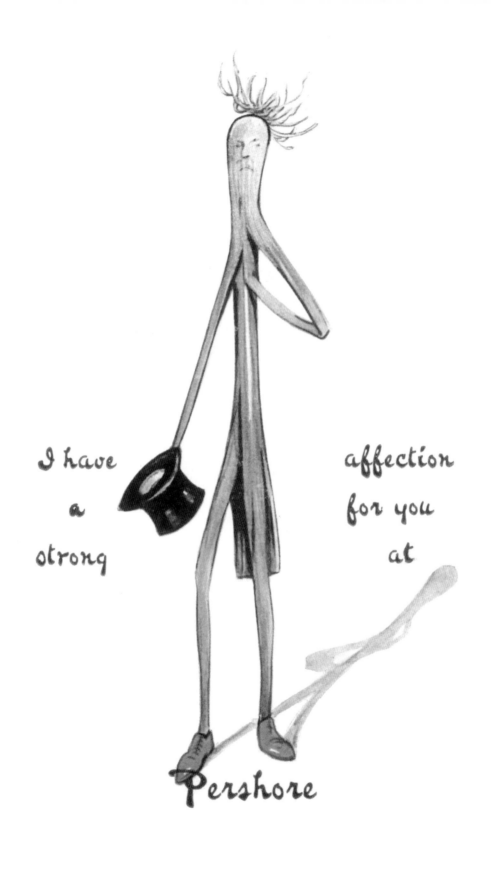

I have a strong

affection for you at

Pershore

IMAGES OF ENGLAND

PERSHORE
REVISITED

MARION FREEMAN

TEMPUS

Frontispiece: A popular type of postcard at the beginning of the twentieth century was one relating to specific towns, large or small. In addition to those featuring views were many humorous cards, often referring to particular aspects for which the town was noted. The Vale of Evesham, where Pershore lies, has for centuries been at the centre of the horticultural industry, as referenced in this postcard.

.

First published 2005

Tempus Publishing Limited
The Mill, Brimscombe Port,
Stroud, Gloucestershire, GL5 2QG
www.tempus-publishing.com

© Marion Freeman, 2005

British Library Cataloguing in Publication Data.
A catalogue record for this book is available from the British Library.

ISBN 0 7524 3737 2

Typesetting and origination by Tempus Publishing Limited.
Printed in Great Britain.

Contents

Acknowledgements

I have spent many happy hours chatting to local folk about the past, browsing through books and researching at the Worcester Record Office. My thanks must therefore go to everyone who has given me information and/or loaned photographs for inclusion in this book

Thanks go to Abbey Park Middle and First School, Mr P. Booth, Mr W. Champken, Cherry Orchard First School, Mr R. Hampton, Mrs M. Marshall, Mr K. Mumford, Mrs M. Payne, Mrs S. Sanders, Mrs J. Simpson, and Mrs L. Tacy. Thanks also to the following for the loan of material: Mr J. Blore, the late Barbara Cartland, Mesdames B. Chalkley and S. Clasen, Mr C. Couchman, Mr B. Davis, Mr and Mrs D. Edwards, Mrs C. Fell, Mrs N. Fletcher, Mr R. Fuller, Mrs Hyder, Mr R. Jaynes, Mrs M. Ludlow, Mr M. Meikle, Number 8, Mr J. Palfrey, Mr T. Parks, Mrs R. Partridge, Pershore Civic Society, Pershore Heritage and History Society, Mr J. Ranford, Mrs M. Ricketts, Mr and Mrs A. Taylor, Father J. Walsh, West Mercia Police, Mr S. Widdowson, Dr M. Wilson, Mrs and Miss P. Winkett, Mr G. Winkett, Worcester Record Office.

Special thanks go to Newsquest and their associated newspapers: *Evesham Journal*, *Worcester Evening News*, and *Berrows Journal*.

Introduction

On the day I moved to Pershore with my family in 1972 I walked to the shops. En route I passed several people, all of whom smiled and said 'Good Morning'. I was amazed – that had never happened in Surbiton! Thus began a love affair with the town, which has grown and expanded over the years. As an avid postcard collector I soon began to amass a collection of cards relating to the town, and I found myself wanting to find out more about Pershore and its past

The information contained in this book has come from many sources, as will be seen from the long list of acknowledgements and the bibliography. So many folk have assisted me by recalling memories and patiently replying to my many queries. In addition, I have been greatly helped by the photographic records of Pershore Civic Society and also information and pictures owned by the Pershore Heritage and History Society, of which I am a founder member and currently the Chairman. There are certain photographs that have obviously been copied over the years and it is now impossible to tell their origins. I suspect that among these are pictures taken by some of our past local photographers: Joseph Glover, William Dowty, and C. Couchman. To these folk the whole town owes a debt for they have captured the spirit of our past in a way that would have been impossible without their work.

Those of you who have seen my earlier book, *Pershore*, in this series will recall that, having begun researching, so much information came to hand that the whole project has become an ongoing one – almost an obsession! While the occasional scene shown in this book is similar to some in the previous book, most of the images have not previously been published. Those that have are included because I felt they deserved a second showing. It is a fact, however, that folk remember events differently and if you feel I have misrepresented anything, do please contact me. I'll be pleased to receive any additional comments or information – after all, having lived in the town for thirty-three years I am still very much a 'foreigner'! Having said that, I've never once been made to feel as such, the town and its people have welcomed me with open arms and I hope it won't be too long before I can regard myself as a local!

Marion Freeman
August 2005

Bibliography

Worcester Sects, John Noakes, 1861
The Rambler in Worcestershire, John Noakes, 1848
Pershore: A Short History, Wilson, Crichton, Johnston, Barrett, 1972
The Book of Pershore, Barrett and Wilson, 1980
RAF Pershore: A History, Glyn Warren, 1982
Yesterday Town: Pershore, Christine Trollope, 1986
A Portrait in Old Picture Postcards, M. Freeman, 1991
Gateway to the Avon, Lower Avon Navigation Trust, 1992
Pershore Abbey Guide, Marshall Wilson, 1994
Images of England: Pershore, M. Freeman, 1997
Pershore Pubs, Past and Present, Janet Daniels, 2002
Evesham '150' Pershore, J. Palfrey and W. Widdowson, 2002
Pershore People, Janet Daniels and Marion Freeman, 2004

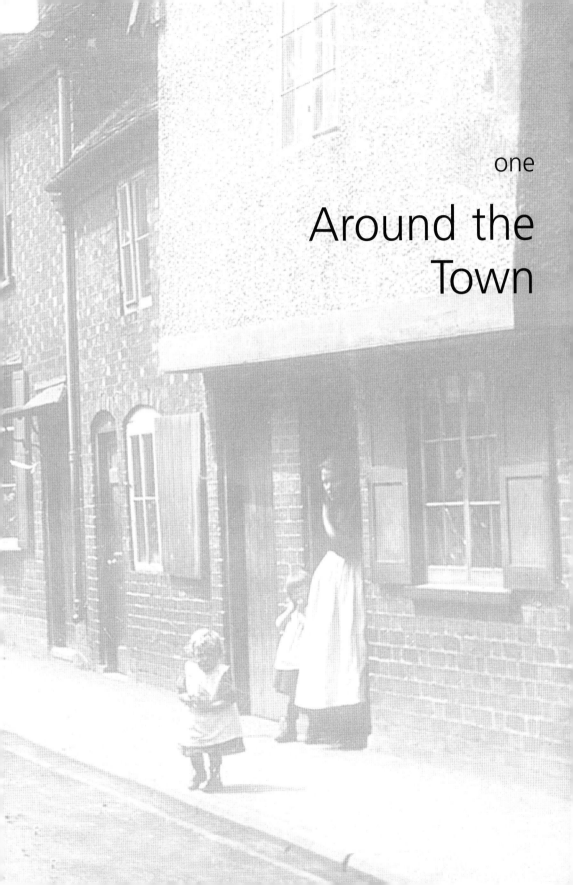

one

Around the Town

The road entering Pershore from Evesham is part of the old London to Aberystwyth road, a journey which took some twenty-four hours by stagecoach; Pershore being situated more or less half way. Avonbank stands on the right at the top of the hill, with Wick House to the left further down. The lodge, home to the coachman, stood at the entrance to the driveway. Both Wick House and the lodge have since been demolished. The motorbike and sidecar were owned by Mr Joseph Glover, the photographer.

Avonbank was the residence of the Marriott family until 1940, and a favourite spot for taking photographs since it granted a panoramic view of the town. There are therefore many variations of this scene but this postcard, posted in 1907, also shows osier beds by the riverbank from which withies were taken for the weaving of fruit hampers. It is said these were planted by Mr Hudson, the owner of Wick House, to shield the view of the village from his home.

The Old and New Bridges, Pershore.

Pershore's two bridges. The main road originally took a much sharper bend at the foot of the hill before crossing the old bridge, which itself was very narrow with pedestrian refuges along the sides. In 1926 a new bridge was erected and inaugurated by Worcester County Council under the chairmanship of Lt-Col. C.F. Milward, the Chairman of the Highways and Bridges Committee. On 23 October 1998 the area was officially opened as a picnic site with notices relating the history, flora and fauna of the surroundings.

A postcard from 1966 showing the river view towards Eckington. The boatyard belonged to Mr J. Sanders, boat builder, who, in addition, hired out boats and launches by the hour or day. It is said he once hired one to Laurel and Hardy while they were staying in the town, reputedly at the Three Tuns Hotel. In 1758 George Perrott purchased the stretch of river from Tewkesbury to Evesham, spending some £4,000 in its restoration, and bringing prosperity to the town through river trade. In 1871 Charles Byrd of Evesham introduced passenger steamers that took trippers for rides on the river.

This postcard, posted in 1916, shows an unusually low water level in the vicinity of the weir. Normally the water was much deeper at this point, tempting unwary swimmers. Local folk had designated bathing points further down river, since to bathe at this spot was quite dangerous. There were many drowning accidents and during the war several airmen based at Wick airfield perished there. On 14 October 1972 a new swimming pool was opened, obtained mainly through the collecting efforts of local residents.

In the early days of detergents a foam-like soap was included in their manufacture. This enabled pranksters to enjoy emptying packets of the substance into various watery outlets such as fountains and ponds. This photograph, taken in 1960, shows a similar event in Pershore lock.

Taken in the late 1950s this photograph shows the side of the Toll House. Such buildings existed on all major roads, and were let out at an annual public auction, although in practice the same person often continued in service for several years. In 1854 this was a Mr Joseph Masters. In exchange for the right to collect tolls he was obliged to maintain the roads and bridge and keep strict accounts. There are several examples of Serpentine walls in the town (the central passageway seen here). Walls erected in this way are stronger, therefore necessitating only one layer of bricks, while spaces in the curves are ideal for sheltering early fruit blossoming trees.

Many of the buildings in Bridge Street (known as Lowel or Lovewell Street in the sixteenth century) still retain at the back, the original medieval buildings which, during Georgian times were updated, presenting a uniform façade fronting the street. Number 39 is one of these. In the basement of the Georgian part of the building are beams, still showing barnacles and nails, signs of their earlier use as shipping bulkheads, thought to have come from a ship breaker's yard at Worcester.

This view of Bridge Street looking towards the bridge clearly shows one of the early gas lamps. Thanks partly to Mr Edwin Ball, a local solicitor (1819-67), gas street-lighting arrived in Pershore in October 1853. *Berrows Journal* in that year wrote of 'jollifications to celebrate the lighting up for the first time of the streets of the town' when 'more than seventy gentry and tradesmen dined together at the Bell Inn, High Street'.

The drawing room of Stanhope House, seen here in the 1950s. The house was built in 1760 by George Perrott for a nephew, another George who was also his accountant, but who never actually lived there, moving to Craycombe House, Fladbury. Stanhope House also included an adjacent building (later Ley School) and many outbuildings, including pigsties, fowl houses, dairy and still rooms. Ley School and its outbuildings were split from the main house in 1934 when purchased by Dr and Mrs Fleming.

The upper end of Bridge Street looking towards the bridge. Beneath the board on the wall of the building on the left-hand side of the street is the old fire station. Its bell would summon the retained firemen to duty, while the horses to pull the engine were kept in fields by the river. To the right is the Royal Three Tuns Hotel on the corner of Broad Street. The prefix Royal was added following a visit by Princess Victoria (later Queen) and her mother, the Duchess of Kent, who made a short stay there in 1830 while on a visit to Malvern.

An early photograph of Broad Street (earlier called Brode Street) showing a fruit market. Prior to around 1836 six houses stood at the eastern end of the street, providing a pleasant open area when demolished. This formed an ideal spot for holding the market and other events. The newly formed Co-Operative Fruit Market held their first sale on 17 June 1909, which proved much more efficient than previously when odd sales of fruit and vegetables had taken place. In 1910 new auction sheds were opened in Defford Road.

Broad Street in the 1950s. To the left is Littleton and Badsey Growers' shop with a yard behind. This replaced Ganderton Row (or Yard) which was demolished, following the Second World War, along with several similar places including Reddings Yard, Church Street and Hall's Entry, Newlands. The trees, with careful pollarding, survived well over a hundred years until they were recently replaced.

Little is known about this photograph of a horse and dray taken in Broad Street sometime in the 1950s. It could be part of a carnival, since the children appear to be in fancy dress. The annual carnival began as a fundraiser to construct a swimming pool in the town which, after much hard work, eventually came to fruition when the pool was opened on a site near the river on 14 October 1972, the town's millennium year.

Broad Street's wide thoroughfare allowed the attractive Georgian architecture to be seen to advantage and it became the hub of the town. There were several suggestions as to its use including, in 1909, the building of a market hall and assembly rooms at an estimated cost of £3,000. This was to have been built at the far end, in the area which had sometimes been called the Forum. With the increase in motor vehicles, including coaches, parking was allowed in the centre of the street.

The wide avenue was also an ideal spot for holding fairs and parades. Here brownies and guides take part in a St George's Day parade in 1958, marching into Broad Street from the then A44 and passing the saluting base.

This postcard, posted in February 1907 shows the foot of Newlands, opposite the Almonry, a medieval house built on the site of the original Abbey Almonry. In the foreground is Godfrey's coal depot. Next door lived Mr Dufty and next to him was Bick's the butcher alongside the 'Drunkard's Lock-Up', where it is reported Ann Bick kept her meat in the 1860s claiming it was 'as good as an icehouse'. The shop was later taken over by Sid Annis.

Slightly further up Newlands, at the end of Little Priest Lane, was the White Hart Inn. It was later run as a corner shop before being demolished in 1969. In 1974 *Berrows Journal* reported evidence of a Roman settlement found by archaeologists excavating in the area.

A view of the same date, showing a lady and child crossing Newlands. The near block of buildings originally belonged to Mr Palfrey with the far grocery shop being taken over by Mr Harding on the death of the former. Across Newlands can be seen the corner of a hairdressing shop and in the distance the old school which later saw service as the public library. Following the construction of the new building the space was used by Gardner's as the foundation of the pickle manufacturing firm.

Behind the hairdressers in Newlands a 200-year-old barn stood until 1985 when permission was granted for a house and bungalow to be built on the spot. Research by the present owner revealed there had been a pond nearby known as Crow Pool. The barn's earlier owners had kept a horse and cart with which they carried fruit from their land around Stocking Brook (now known as Bow Brook).

Top end of Newlands looking towards the Abbey. The children sitting in the doorway are the Haynes children. One day while playing in the street they were approached by Barbara Cartland who lived at Amerie Court opposite, asking if they would like some of her toys. The thought was a kind one, but by prefacing the request by saying 'Poor children, would you like…' the offer was refused and the gifts thrown back over the wall!

Members of the Haynes family outside the back of the same cottage. Newlands, while always in the 'New Land' area, had sometimes been known as Mailcoach Road as the coach travelling to and from Worcester took this route.

This postcard, dated 6 April 1910, shows the corner of Broad Street and High Street. At this time the corner shop was known as Pershore Supply Stores. Next door was the surgery of Dr Wilson, and adjacent to it the hardware shop belonging to Mr F. Greenhous, later taken over by Mr Broome before becoming the Co-Op shop.

Heavy storms in June 1921 caused floods in Priest Lane and the High Street. This view shows a waterlogged street outside the Ship Inn where the Go Down stands today. In 1817 the owner was Honeybourne Workman, a butcher, but by the time this photograph was taken, the licensee was probably Alfred Adams who was there for nine years.

Numbers 101–103 High Street. The houses to the right were demolished when Cherry Orchard Road was formed. One of the children is thought to be Kathleen Dancocks (later Evans) with her elder sister Winifred.

Opposite the Plough, one of the oldest inns in the town, Priest Lane leads from the High Street to the Abbey. This street is still sometimes called Plough Lane by locals. Although many of these houses, including the one on the corner, have been updated and renovated (and several disappeared altogether) it's possible to identify today's buildings with these earlier ones. Beyond the folk standing in the middle of the street can be seen the back of the White Horse pub.

Mr J.W. Smith standing outside his house in Priest Lane, where he carried out the business of builder and undertaker. When he died at the end of the First World War, the business was taken over by his son Will. This continued until his death when it was sold, and the site is now occupied by the Health Centre. Will lived in the High Street and had a tobacco and sweet shop where Superdrug now stands.

In 1934 a new drill hall was erected in Defford Road, at a cost of £2,200, and opened in January 1914 by Lord Coventry. Among the builders was Mr Smith. When the building was taken over as the Fire Station and Ambulance Centre the imposing entrance, seen here in construction, was replaced by large doors allowing the passage of fire engines to be garaged there.

CHURCH STREET PERSHORE.

Above and left: Church Street had earlier been known as Lich Street, Lych Lane or Leech Street. These three cottages (*left*) in the middle of the street can also be seen at the far end of the street in the above photograph. By 1957 they were in a derelict state and it was ruled they should be demolished. They were purchased by Mr Winkett and Frank Bartlett for the sum of £300. It was later discovered that the roofs were heavily leaded, almost paying for their cost. The old beams were sold and the bricks saved and used to build sixteen garages backing on to the wall of the White Horse Inn.

The Hall, Station Road, also called the Mount. This was built in 1862 by Edward Humphries who, with his brother Thomas, in 1840, set up an agricultural machinery works in the High Street, later moving to a site near Pershore station. By 1909 William Deakin was living here surrounded by farmland and orchards growing fruit to supply his jam factories at Wigan and Farrington. He later established a tinning factory at Norton, where until recently the tall chimney associated with the factory could be seen.

Several gardeners were employed at The Hall to work in the extensive grounds which included a tennis court and pool.

This view of the town taken from the rise on the Worcester side, clearly shows the abbey, at a time when the Abbey Estate was being built, when it and the Bowling Club were surrounded by fruit orchards, grazing and market-garden land. The newly constructed Abbey Road can be seen with Farleigh Road leading into it.

When this aerial view of the town was taken in the late 1940s, early 1950s, it appears that both Ganderton Row and Batchelor's Entry had been demolished. On the left-hand side the row of pre-fabricated buildings erected at the end of the war and demolished in 1970, which fronted Abby Road, can be seen. Also clearly seen is the back of the Baptist church and, by then, the well established fruit and vegetable market in Defford Road.

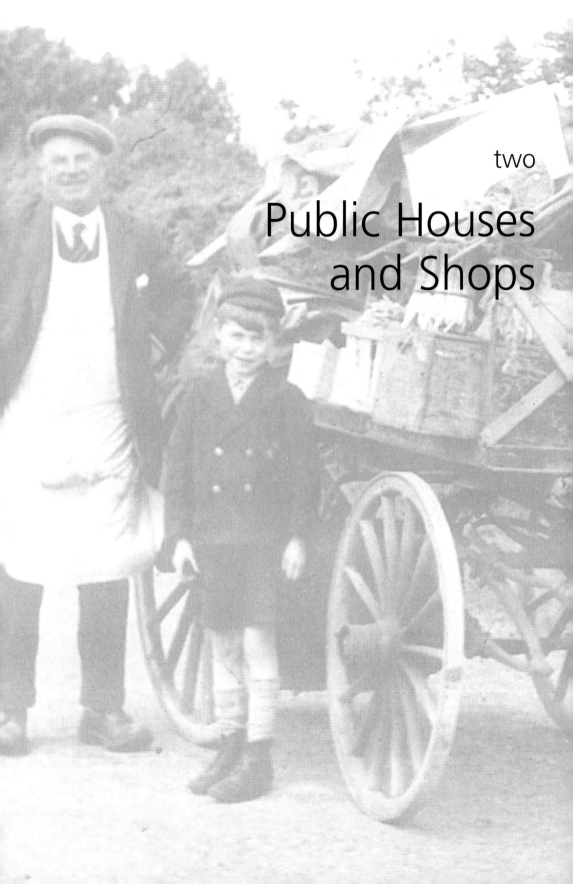

two

Public Houses
and Shops

Above: The car at the corner outside the Three Tuns Hotel, appears to be chauffeur driven. Could this be that belonging to the author Francis Brett Young of Fladbury, who was often seen being driven around the town in the early days of motoring? In 1830 when Royalty stayed here, the inn would have been a thatched building. This was one of the main coaching inns on the London to Worcester route and in the early twentieth century was much used as a meeting place for a variety of organisations.

Left: Advertisement for the Three Tuns Hotel.

ASSEMBLY OR BALL ROOM AT
ROYAL THREE TUNS HOTEL, PERSHORE.

Above: This postcard view, posted on
6 August 1907, shows the hotel ballroom
with windows opening on to the veranda
and looking into Broad Street. Grand
balls were held here, including, in 1909, a
Cinderella dance in connection with the
Tradesmen's Dancing Class. The inaugural
meeting of Pershore & District Fruit &
Market Growers was held here in April
1907 when the proprietor was M.W. Bird.

Right: The main entrance to the hotel
looking towards the coaching windows on
the right-hand side at the far end.

ANGEL HOTEL

A 1950s photograph of Bridge Street showing The Star and the Brandy Cask pubs. The Star Inn, its entrance surmounted by a golden star, was at one time called the Coach and Horses; a coaching inn under the proprietorship of Thomas Featherstone, with stabling for ninety horses. During the early 1850s Mormon missionaries (Church of Jesus Christ of Latter Day Saints) were very active in the area and held Sunday meetings at the Star that were apparently poorly attended. In 1963 Frank and Chris Swan took over the licence. Many of the businesses whose property backed onto the river would hire out rowing boats and there has long been a mooring space at the back of the Swan. The Brandy Cask, a Tudor building with a Georgian frontage, was originally a wool warehouse, and like its next-door neighbour, also had a later change of name. Known as the Liquor Vaults, the Baker family bottled their own wines, spirits and beer, distributing it by horse and cart to local large houses. The first landlord was S.O. Collett, an ex-policeman. The grounds to both hotels reach to the river and have attractive gardens, while the Brandy Cask has its own brewery, built in 1995, at the rear of the premises. These Bitter beers, brewed using traditional methods are much prized.

Opposite above: The High Street looking towards Worcester. Opposite the Old Corner shop stands the Angel Inn and Posting House whose entrance was reached through the adjacent archway. Like several of the older inns in the town this was used as a gathering place for various organisations including the Vale of Evesham Road Club and the Freemasons. It also had a large ballroom to the rear.

Opposite below: Little is known of the early history of the Angel but it is of Tudor origin and Queen Elizabeth is said to have stayed there. A portrait of an Elizabethan woman was revealed on a wall when alterations were made in 1922 and the place is said to be haunted by a man in naval dress.

A publicity drawing of The Star, *c*. 1950.

A view taken from the river showing the rear of the Star Hotel, *c*. 1950. Earlier, under the proprietorship of Alfred Hicken, attractive gardens had reached the banks of the river and the hotel had managed a thriving business hiring out and storing boats of various types both to individuals and boating parties.

Right: The Black Swan Public House, a three-storey Elizabethan building stood at No. 54 Bridge Street (near Bedford house) behind the present antique shop. It had ceased to be used as a pub for many years, and during the war was occupied by evacuees, one of whom swore she'd seen a ghost there. When major improvements were undertaken in the town, and the majority of the substandard housing removed, the then owner of the property was told he must either renovate or remove this building. Grants being unavailable in 1964 he was obliged to demolish it, finding when he did that it was very well constructed, so much so that he broke two circular saws on the beams. In the fireplace he found some medieval coins, presumably put there to discourage evil spirits.

Below: Old windows revealed during the demolition.

The Black Horse, situated on the corner of Priest Lane and Church Row, is known to have been in existence, since at least 1840, when James Freeman owned a beerhouse on the premises. His wife Sarah held the licence by 1855. The building finally closed as a licensed premises on 29 November 1967 when it was sold by Flowers Brewery as a private house.

There is still evidence of wattle and daub and an old walk-in fireplace at The Talbot in the Newlands. This public house had a series of titles: known earlier as The Malthouse; in the seventeenth century it became The Swan; and an 1855 directory shows it as the Waterloo Tavern. When it became The Talbot is unclear. It is believed that Civil War soldiers were billeted here and there are tales of a ghost of a Royalist soldier being seen. Detailed histories of all Pershore's pubs can be found in Janet Daniel's book (*see* Bibliography).

Above: This photograph of Barclays Bank in Bridge Street was taken in the 1950s and shows the magnificent Georgian frontage. At the time of building, there were various brochures in existence from which owners could choose the type of fanlight that could be used above their front door. Those in Bridge Street showed a variety of styles, and were presumably dependent upon the preference and affordability of the owners. Next door to Barclays Bank can be seen the doors to the original fire station.

Right: Taken around the same time as the previous photograph, this splendid staircase led to the upper floors in the bank. In 1931 the Manager was Mr E.H. Parry.

The London Joint City and Midland Bank, later known as the Midland Bank, was still being called by its earlier name in 1912 while under the management of Mr A.C. Goddard. Now known as HSBC, the bank originally occupied only the right-hand side of the building, with a ladies' outfitters and drapers to the left. In 1931 the Manager was Mr Leonard Terrell Bayley.

Taken in the 1950s, this photograph shows the drawing room on the first floor of the Midland Bank building.

Right: This Christmastime scene, from around 1903, shows the fish and poultry shop owned by Jack Pritchard, who is seen standing near the house. Jack's brother, Will, is on the right with another brother, Grenville, at the back. He later became a missionary, dying in Africa shortly after having arrived there. The shop stood in the High Street near the Arcade, which was until recently the premises of the shoe shop Tappers', and is now part of the hairdresser's, Sweeny Todd.

Below: Mr John Pritchard standing with his loaded cart from which he sold vegetables and fish around Pershore and the nearby villages, *c.* 1930.

Fearnside newsagent and bookseller in Bridge Street. The Avon Printing Works was part of this business and, in addition to printing illuminated addresses, testimonials, *in memoriam* cards and other printed matter, every year produced a diary and directory known as 'The Blue Book'. This contained an illustrated almanac of interesting features, useful local information, and a diary of the principal local events of the year. The shop existed until the early 1970s when it was taken over by Dillons. More recently it has become a hairdresser's.

In 1973, the building housing the old fire station with its arched doorway was sympathetically converted to a shop selling high-class ladies' clothing. Later, after having served as offices to a building firm, it became the Town Council office, until they moved to the present Town Hall two years ago. The doorway to the right led into a passageway in which stood the front door of the adjacent house. This (No. 5 Bridge Street) later became the home of the Pershore Heritage and History Society, opened in 1995, which is now housed within the Town Hall premises.

Above and below: Two views showing the corner of Broad Street and High Street. The shop was also known as Prothero & Co., Burton and Fine Fare. With each new proprietor the frontage was updated, and bus shelters had been installed in Broad Street by the 1960s.

To the left of the Three Tuns Hotel was a draper's shop belonging to Peter Hanson (1846-1932), known as the 'Mayor of Pershore' by the locals. The property was then owned by Dick Edwards who removed a first-floor bay window. The frontage was again updated in 1966 following the taking of this photograph when the property became Gerrard's, before eventually becoming Seal's, selling ladies' and gent's clothing. More recently it became an IT centre organised by the Horticultural College, but in August 2005 returned to its former use as a clothing shop.

Opposite the end of Broad Street stood the ironmonger's shop belonging to W.L. Brown, known to locals to sell 'just about everything in the hardware line'. Next door stood Budd's the chemist, who had taken over from Mr Smith who made up his own pills and ointments. The Willow Café, adjacent to this, was in the hands of Miss Spiers who lived there with her two brothers, Jim, a haircutter working in Christine's, and Ben. She served meals in addition to morning coffee and afternoon tea and was known by her friends for her Boxing Night parties.

Number 8 High Street was built in 1741 and began life as a candle factory. In 1954 the Co-operative Society, who had earlier opened a store on the corner of Priest Lane and High Street, moved to the site of Greenhous ironmongery, nearer Broad Street. Later the building underwent further modernisation when square windows were inserted and a side entrance formed, as shown in the lower photograph. During the early 1990s the building remained empty for some years, although it was used for part of that time as a YMCA charity shop. In 1996, a steering group was set up to develop the site as a theatre and arts centre. The project became a registered charity, the Pershore Theatre & Arts Group, and extensive fundraising was undertaken by a committee of enthusiastic volunteers.

The group redecorated the building and divided it into a series of rooms for use by various organisations with a film club, meeting at the weekend, that gained a membership of around 800. During this interim period, the front of the premises was used as a charity shop in order to raise more funds.

Under the lead of Ray Steadman and Jane Daniels with an extensive band of volunteers and unstinting support from the townspeople, the new venue is now the pride and joy of the town, showing films, hosting live programmes and providing a vast variety of activities for all ages. The entrance leads into an attractive and spacious foyer where drinks and refreshments can be obtained, and in addition to the auditorium there are rooms where a variety of arts and crafts are carried out.

The initial impetus for the project had come from the Pershore Operatic and Dramatic Society, which had been formed in 1989 under the leadership of Stuart and Judy Megarry, many of their members becoming fully involved with the new undertaking. They became the resident Amateur Theatre Group at the new building and it was therefore fitting they presented the opening show entitled *Show Stoppers!* on 4 December 2005.

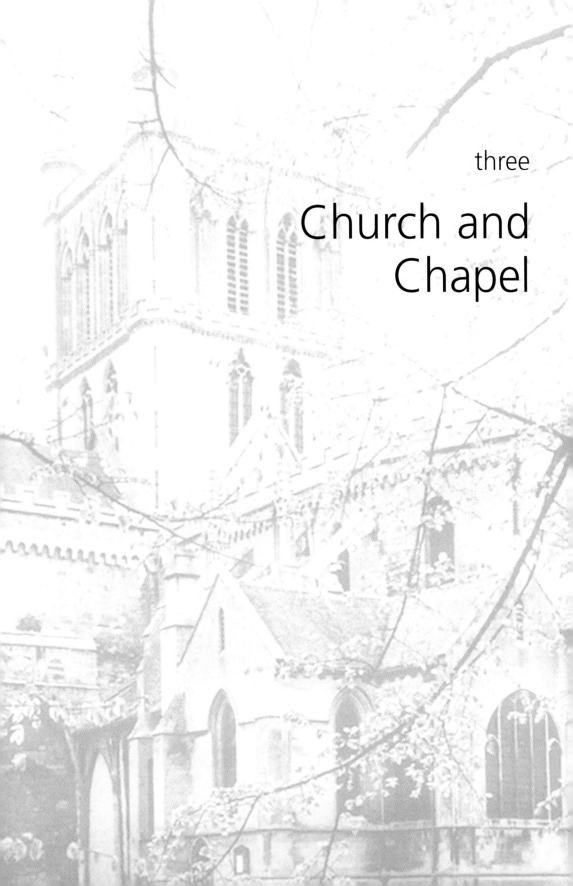

three

Church and Chapel

A rare early photograph of Pershore Abbey, showing the roofline of the original north transept and tiny blocked access door to the roof. The Abbey was first mentioned in AD 681 when an endowment from Ethelred, King of Mercia, provided a religious house, and within eight years there was a monastic community in the town. The Abbey was dedicated to St Eadburga, a grand-daughter of King Alfred. In AD 792 the Benedictine rule was introduced. In 1540, during the Reformation, the Abbey was surrendered to the King, the monks in the main continuing as priests in nearby villages. While most of the former monastery was demolished, the parishioners purchased the former monks' choir for use as their parish church. Following the collapse of the north transept, a stabilising buttress was erected in 1686. In the 1860s the architect Gilbert Scott was employed to restore the building. He opened up the lantern tower exposing the attractive internal panelling. Pinnacles were added to the tower in 1871 as thanks, it is said, to Worcester glove-makers in appreciation of the fine work undertaken by Pershore outworkers.

A postcard, dated 30 August 1935, showing the south transept, the oldest part of Pershore Abbey. Here, the War Memorial dedicated on 1 November 1921, fronts two ancient tombs. One, moved to its present position from the north-east transept, was for some time thought to commemorate a fourteenth-century abbot, William de Harvington, but later research now believes it to be the effigy of Abbot Edmund Hert (1456-79). The other is of a knight in chain armour from the latter part of the thirteenth century, brought in from the churchyard and placed here in 1864. It is of especial interest since it clearly shows how such armour would have been buckled.

A close-up of one of the forty-one bosses in the Abbey vaulting; no two are identical. They are carved in a naturalistic style and among them are several foliated heads, or Green Men, apparently showing a mixture of pagan and Christian ideas. One of the best known of these shows a laughing face framed in foliage.

Above: The two buttresses either side of the west door were erected in 1913, and this aerial view shows the Abbey before the construction of the flagged path from the west door to the gates which were put in place in 1964 and said to have been returned to their origins from Marriott's Bank. These gates mark the original start of the nave. Also shown is St Andrew's church and the vicarage, rebuilt in 1848 by the then vicar, D'Arcy Haggitt.

Left: A lychgate lead to the Abbey at the end of Church Street. This was earlier known as Lych or Leech Street with a mortuary situated at the far end near to High Street. A lychgate (or lichgate) is a gateway, usually with a roof, set at the entrance to the churchyard where the coffin rests awaiting the arrival of the officiating clergyman prior to interment, the word being a combination of 'gate' and Old English '*lic*', meaning a body, whether alive or dead.

In the 1950s, the lychgate was removed, and it was decided to use part of the money bequeathed to the Abbey by the Misses Woodward on the erection of some gates to replace it. These were to be known as the Woodward Gates 'in appreciation of the devotion and generosity of the Woodward family to the Abbey for many years'. At the same time the wall surrounding the churchyard was lowered.

The new Woodward Gates and the lowered wall.

A group of Abbey members taken on an unknown occasion, *c.* 1912. The man second from the right in the third row is believed to be William Smith, with Nancy Matthews sitting fifth from the right, and her sister Maude third from the right in the second row.

Sunday school whist-drive, 28 December 1911.

The Abbey font is one of the most historically interesting items in the building. This Norman lead-lined carved-stone basin is beautifully decorated with an interlacing series of arches, in the panels of which are figures depicting Christ and the apostles. During Victorian times it was removed in favour of a more 'modern' construction and for many years the original served as a cattle trough, eventually being rediscovered in the garden of The Nash in Kempsey where it was being used as a flower container. It was then restored to its rightful place, erected on a pedestal designed by Harold Brakspeare.

A springtime photograph taken by *Warwickshire Life* magazine showing the east end of the Abbey from St Andrew's gardens. From the models of the cars it appears this phototgraph was taken during the late 1960s or early '70s.

In 1955, a stone cross carved in medieval fashion, was dredged from the river near the old Pershore Bridge while work was being carried out by the Lower Avon Navigation Trust to deepen the main channel below the bridge. The cross and its heavy base portion were raised separately but fitted so well together that there was no question that the complete article had been discovered. It is thought it could be part of the Abbey. Following the Dissolution the Abbey was raided as a source of building material – many of the old houses in the town show signs of this. For some years this cross was in the care of the museum at Evesham, who donated it to the Pershore Heritage Society in 1996. It now stands in the walkway by the Town Hall.

Located on the site where the Bowling Club now stands, Abbey House, originally the Bedford family home, became home to a group of Anglican monks from the Caldey Island community in 1914. When, after twelve years, the group had outgrown the premises, they moved to Nashdon in Buckinghamshire, and the house was later demolished.

The chapel at Abbey House.

Above, left: Looking into the drawing room from the black and white marble hall at Abbey House.
Above, right: The staircase at Abbey House.

Another very early photograph showing the north side of St Andrew's church taken from the Abbey grounds. Although rebuilt and restored several times over the centuries, the present structure is mainly fifteenth-century work. It was founded in the reign of Edward the Confessor in the eleventh century when certain abbey lands were transferred to the Abbot of Westminster in order to endow his new Abbey there. This resulted in resentment by Pershore monks angry at the loss of their lands and who, since the townspeople thus became tenants of Westminster, felt they should not continue to worship at the Abbey. Westminster therefore built a new church for the tenants and the town was split into two parishes. After belonging for a while to Great Malvern Priory, St Andrew's was granted to the Abbey in 1327. Following the departure of the monks from the Abbey, St Andrew's became a parish church and remained so until 1961, although regular services stopped in 1943. In 1971 work began to convert it into a parish centre. It is believed King John worshipped here on his way to Worcester.

A postcard view of the south side of St Andrew's, taken from the Abbey. This card was posted on 14 September 1913.

A postcard photograph showing the interior of St Andrew's while in use as a church. When it became a parish centre the south aisle was converted into an entranceway, committee room and kitchen, while the ground floor of the three-stage 12ft-tower became toilets. The nave and north aisle remained much as they were, forming the main hall, and a room, originally the chancel, was formed behind a movable partition, with the vestry to the left. In 1993 part of the roof was destroyed by fire but was soon restored and more recent alterations took place enabling the building to be used even more extensively.

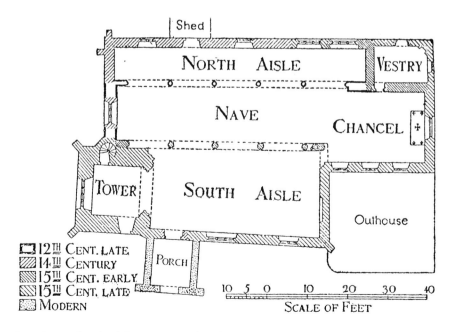

A plan of St Andrew's while in use as a church.

A right-hand view of the High Street, facing Worcester. In the centre a shop window with a circle above can be seen. Next door is now the Arcade Book Shop, whose owner welcomes visitors to the basement which hides a thirteenth-century chapel and undercroft. It is thought this was probably part of a pilgrim's hostelry for visitors to the shrine of St Eadburga at the Abbey, since relics of the saint had been purchased by the Saxon, Earl Odda, and given to the Abbey. It is said that a blind man was cured after bathing his eyes in water in which Eadburga had washed her hands, and following other miracles at her shrine, Pershore became a minor pilgrimage centre.

Reverend Frank Overbury was Baptist minister for some years until 1860. He seems to have been very active in the town, chairing meetings and presenting petitions.

Opposite below: It is believed there may be tunnels running towards the Abbey from the chapel, which is in dressed stone with a piscine (a stone basin used by the priest for washing his hands before and during mass and for cleansing the chalice after use) in the south wall and a trefoil (a symbol of the Holy Trinity) in the west wall. There are also remains of a spiral staircase that apparently ends in a well. It is thought the chapel was used secretly during the seventeenth century by Catholics wishing to adhere to their old religion when the laws of the land decreed attendance at the established church.

The Baptist church is thought to have been founded in 1658, the last year of Cromwell's rule, and is therefore one of the oldest in the country. The church itself is set far back from the road, fronted by other rooms. At the time of its foundation, rules relating to attendance at the established church were still in force so the congregation had its beginnings hidden behind other buildings, in what was probably an old malt house. But by the end of the century they were commanding congregations of some 7-800 'hearers' on Sundays – presumably many from surrounding villages. The site of the church and manse was acquired by Samuel Rickards but when, in 1736, those who believed in infant baptism were excluded from attendance the congregation diminished to only forty-eight members. John Ash became minister around 1749 where he remained for over twenty-eight years.

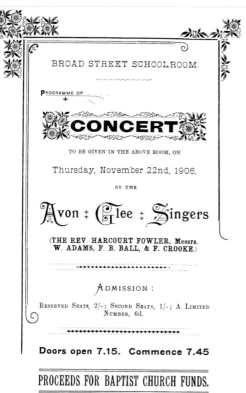

BROAD STREET SCHOOLROOM.

PROGRAMME OF

CONCERT

TO BE GIVEN IN THE ABOVE ROOM, ON

Thursday, November 22nd, 1906,

BY THE

Avon ‡ Glee ‡ Singers

(THE REV. HARCOURT FOWLER, Messrs.
W. ADAMS, F. B. BALL, & F. CROOKE.)

ADMISSION :

RESERVED SEATS, 2/-; SECOND SEATS, 1/-; A LIMITED
NUMBER, 6d.

Doors open 7.15. Commence 7.45

PROCEEDS FOR BAPTIST CHURCH FUNDS.

T. HALL, PRINTER.

Above: Pershore Baptist Sunday School, winners of the Sunday School Union challenge shield, 1912.

Left: A concert programme, organised for an event to raise funds for the Baptist church. This concert, performed in two halves, was given by various members of the town. Mr A.J. Feek played selections on the pianoforte, the Revd H.B.S. Fowler and Mr F.B. Ball rendered songs, also singing a duet together, and the Pershore Glee Party presented a series of quartets.

Father Holly was chaplain to the Berkeley family at Spetchley Park when, one winter's night in 1908, he was called to the aid of a sick woman. This began his wider ministry and he eventually set up a Mass Centre in the warehouse of Phillip's grocers shop in the High Street (the old music hall). Later, he was able to set up a chapel in Priest Lane, using the old iron chapel from Evesham, which was donated when a new church was built there. After working tirelessly, he eventually felt the calling to become a monk at Caldey Island, leaving Pershore on 18 January 1913. Between 1917 and 1943 there was no resident priest in Pershore. During this time, the Catholic congregation was served by priests from Upton upon Severn and Basford Court.

In 1944, Father Charles J. O'Reilly was appointed to Pershore, living at No. 39 High Street in 1946. He started a building fund, having in the meantime persuaded Italian prisoners of war to wire the old chapel for electricity and German prisoners to paint it, by which time there was a local congregation of some 120. In 1955, his successor, Father Edward Burbage, was able to purchase the site in Priest Lane. Father (later Monsignor) James Crichton arrived in November of that year, the foundation stone of the new church was laid on 24 May 1958 and the church opened during Holy Week the following year.

The Society of Friends, or Quakers, dates from around 1650 and was founded by George Fox, who was born in 1624. On 20 July 1662 a meeting was broken up by a party of soldiers who, with swords, forced the people from the building, driving them through the streets to Worcester prison. It appears that by 1664 there was an active Quaker congregation in the town, for seven members were reported by the churchwardens of Holy Cross, with a further seven from St Andrew's. George Fox held meetings here in 1667 and again in 1678, but by 1699 Pershore became part of the Evesham Monthly Meeting, held alternatively at each place. Seven years later, Redditch, Alcester, Leigh Green and Bishampton, four of the more distant gatherings, were also joined to Pershore and Evesham. At meetings, enquiries were made regarding prisoners – how many were held, discharged or had died, also how many new Meeting Houses had been built and whether the poor belonging to the group were being cared for. It is believed the Quaker burial ground was where, until recently, the Central Garage stood on the corner of Head Street and High Street. The Pershore Meeting House was thoroughly repaired in 1779 at a cost of £86.18, but, by 1801, the graveyard was leased as garden ground to Lawyer Bedford. In 1803 it was decided that even the annual gathering be discontinued, and in 1813 the Meeting House itself was disposed of for the sum of £100.

four

Events and Organisations

Pershore's fair was established during the Middle Ages, when rights were granted to the Abbot of Pershore by Henry III in 1266. The fairs were primarily concerned with trade and held annually, and until 1868 householders were allowed to sell beer and cider without licence provided they placed a green bush outside their doors. Over time the commercial element was displaced, leaving the event closer to today's form. Of the three fairs held annually, that most enjoyed was the one around St Eadburga's Day. Held in the churchyard each year on 26 June (the date having changed during the eighteenth century) it retained this site until 1836 when it moved to Broad Street, since by that time it had become a somewhat riotous event. On the evening prior to the fair, traders would stand at the entrances to Broad Street until, at 8 p.m., a local police inspector would give a signal for all to rush for the best pitches, any unlucky punters ending up in Weir Meadow. Around the First World War the popularity of the fair began to wane, ceasing completely with the advent of the Second World War. Today the tradition is carried on by the annual arrival of the funfair at Weir Meadow.

Local girls at the fair in Broad Street.

Early in the twentieth century, Empire Day was actively supported in Pershore with street parades being held. As the years passed the event seemed to be celebrated only in schools where patriotic songs were sung and the children instructed on the greatness of the Empire under Victoria.

May Day celebrations, 31 May 1906. It is not known why this event should have been held so late in the month, for traditionally May Day celebrations took place on 1 May. The early standard maypole, a symbol of virility, could be 60–80ft high and brightly painted, the dance probably beginning as a rite in honour of the sun god, the god of fertility. Village maidens would dance around the pole, the loveliest being chosen as Queen, who was originally thought to have represented Flora, the Roman goddess of Spring.

There was a very active group of the Girls' Life Brigade at the Baptist chapel around 1940. It is believed that from left to right, back row, are: Margaret Potts (?), Meryl Johnson, Dorothy Broome, Helen Cole, Pauline Johnson, Bernice Marshall, Monica Wright, Shirley Robbins, Pat Winkett. Middle row: Gaynor Paddon, Glenda Cosnett, June Roberts, Mary Gould, Mrs Poole, Mr Johnson, Mrs Johnson, Nurse Monks, Barbara Cornelius, Myrna Young, Yvonne Lambert. Front row: Pat Poole, Josephine Cole, -?-, -?-, Nancy Cole, Janet Ball, Betty Drinkwater, Hilary Marshall, Wendy Champken, Janet Ball.

There was a group of Scouts in the town by 1909, but this photograph in the *Berrow's Worcester Journal* free supplement of 13 May 1911 shows an inspection of Fladbury, Cropthorne and Charlton Troop Scouts that took place in Pershore. The Troop met in a number of places around the town, including the drill hall and the old National School, the Baptist schoolroom and a loft at the rear of a shop that became the old Co-Operative furniture store. In the 1950s they were able to move to a permanent home in King George's Way, which was recently demolished and is now the site of the Princess Diana Memorial Garden.

The 1st Pershore Brownie Pack in 1925. It is not known who the Brown Owl was at this time but the District Captain was Miss Joan Elkington. By 1987 the Brown Owl was Miss Esther Marshall.

It is unknown when this photograph was taken or who the girls are, but it appears to be the cook patrol preparing a meal at camp.

There had been a couple of exhibitions of bulb flowers held in the Three Tuns Hotel, but a public meeting heralded the formation of the Pershore Horticultural and Floral Association; the first show taking place in the Abbey grounds (then owned by Miss Bedford) on 29 July 1875. Public subscriptions enabled good prizes to be awarded for both the show and its attendant entertainments. Held in the Abbey grounds, a wooden stand was erected for spectators, with runners attending from such prestigious clubs as the Birchfield Harriers. A large marquee was also erected. Various bands entertained during the afternoon, church bells rang and the day concluded with a grand firework display. The second year the date was changed to August bank holiday, and continued to be held in August for the remainder of its duration. Over the years, the event grew from strength to strength, and when, in 1884, they combined with the Worcestershire Agricultural Society to hold a three-day event, over 10,000 people attended. This joint venture was not continued but the 1909 event saw over 800 horticultural entries alone. The last recorded show took place in 1913, although it was reinstated for a short period at the beginning of 1951 and 1961. In 1989 the event again became an annual one, but 2005 saw its demise due to an appropriate venue being unavailable.

For several years a Donkey Derby was a part of the Flower Show event. Here we see the event in 1911.

Above: The officials and committee responsible for organising the Flower Show in the early 1900s.

Right: By 1883, the Bedford family had moved from the Abbey grounds. However, their successors allowed the Flower Show to continue to be held there. In connection with this were a series of other events, each programme containing a report of the previous year. We learn therefore that in 1882 'the weather was favourable, the large number of visitors passing through the gates fully making up for the increased expenditure'. The competent judges ruled that the 'fruit and vegetables were magnificent, not excelled at any of the principal shows in the kingdom'. The Band of the Grenadiers delighted all lovers of music, the Athletic Sports attracted a large number of competitors and the fireworks and illumination of the Abbey gateway, by means of Venetian lanterns, were highly successful. Prize winners were requested to attend the music hall on Saturday 11 August.

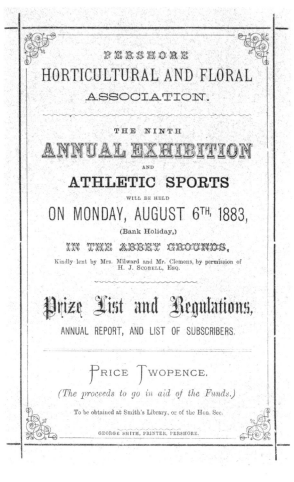

PERSHORE

HORTICULTURAL AND FLORAL
ASSOCIATION.

THE NINTH

ANNUAL EXHIBITION
AND

ATHLETIC SPORTS

WILL BE HELD

ON MONDAY, AUGUST 6TH, 1883,
(Bank Holiday,)

IN THE ABBEY GROUNDS.

Kindly lent by Mrs. Milward and Mr. Clemens, by permission of
H. J. SCOBELL, ESQ.

Prize List and Regulations,

ANNUAL REPORT, AND LIST OF SUBSCRIBERS.

PRICE TWOPENCE.

(The proceeds to go in aid of the Funds.)

To be obtained at Smith's Library, or of the Hon. Sec.

GEORGE SMITH, PRINTER, PERSHORE.

In 1922, some fifty players took part in 'Living Bridge' produced by Nancy Matthews, Head of Drakes Broughton School. The lady players were dressed in long white dresses and the men in tunics with a ruff about their necks. This photograph, taken some ten years later, shows a similar event, 'Living Whist', organised by the WI and produced by the President, Mrs Rusher. Dressed appropriately, the 'cards' were shuffled to music, children taking the part of the lower cards in the suit.

Following the Second World War a new dramatic society was formed under their President, Dr Neville Hind. Performing over two days some 700 members of the audience enjoyed the play the *Chiltern Hundreds* by Douglas Hume at the Plaza cinema. The cast are, from left to right: Alex Melvin (Lord Cleghorn), Mildred Melvin (Lady Caroline Smith), Katherine Colori (Countess of Lister), Jim Gardner (Beecham), David Howell (Earl of Lister), Dorothy Hunt (June Farrel), Effie Palfrey (Bessie) and Walter Palfrey (Lord Pym).

Publicity notice situated at the far end of Broad Street advertising the 1969 Pershore Festival. This arts event was inaugurated by Dr Peter Moore who, as vicar under the patronage of Sir George Dowty, was enthusiastically supported by a large group of helpers. The first festival was held in 1961, when it was 'hoped it may become an annual event', which it did for some years, continuing until the 1980s. During the week-long event, a large variety of special musical concerts, plays, exhibitions and social events took place at varying venues throughout the town.

Each year a play was produced, performed by the Festival Players under the direction of Bob Ashworth, the Deputy Headmaster at the High School. In 1961 it was *Murder in the Cathedral* by T.S. Eliot where the part of Archbishop Thomas Becket was played by Revd John Hencher, supported by a cast of twenty-five. The following year a play, *The Wanderer*, was specially written for the Abbey.

In the 1960s, Wick WI responded to an appeal by the Lower Avon Navigation Trust to raise funds for the repair of Avon Locks, which was incorporated on 1 August 1950. Many major works have been carried out since that time, accomplished entirely by voluntary fundraising, and in 1961 the Navigation was re-opened all the way to Evesham. This photograph shows the committee of the WI at a meeting held at Wick Grange. Names include Mesdames Brigdale, Bramford, Savage, Parkes, Hine, Cosnett, Mr C. Meikle, Horton, Mrs M.A. Meikle (president), Wilson, Bramfield, Rees, Baxter, Knott, Burford.

Pershore WI will be celebrating their ninetieth birthday in 2006, having been formed in 1916 under the presidency of Mrs Geoffrey Hooper. Since its formation it has organised and taken part in a host of varying activities and fundraising events. This photograph, taken by Mr Couchman around 1960, shows a scene from a pageant entitled 'Fashion Past & Present'. Those taking part are believed to be, from left to right: -?-, C. Fraser, R. Brant, -?-, F. Baldwin, D. Brant, M. Jevons, A. Vint, V. Evans.

Pershore has always been an extremely active town with a great many organisations, both local and national. Among the latter have been such groups as the Boot and Shoemakers Society, Penny Readings, the Women's Unionist Society, and the Pig Keepers' Association. The Bowling Club has a long and impressive history, having been formed in 1928 following an invitation by the then Lord Abbot of Pershore to tradesmen of the town to play bowls on the monastery lawn. He became president, continuing until the monks left in 1936, with Frank Boswell the first Captain. The Club began in a small way with two rinks, but following the Second World War expanded to six rinks with a ladies section formed in 1953.

The League of Pity was a charity that undertook fundraising on behalf of deprived children. Members saved change in special boxes, taking these with them to meetings to be collected, opened and counted. Parties took place in the ballrooms at both the Three Tuns and the Angel Hotels.

The original Pershore Working Men's club was started in 1877 when Archdeacon Walters was vicar, with meetings being held in a house in Newlands. In 1884 the club moved to premises in the High Street where it had free use of ground at the back for athletic sports. Thanks to donations from Mrs Marriott, Mrs Evans, Bryn Issa and Miss Martin, supported by Mr Alfred Hudson of Wick House, the present property was purchased in 1887 and its ownership vested in Trustees. The inauguration of the new premises took place on 20 October that year and was celebrated by a free tea to members, followed by a concert. The original premises contained a hall and committee room but following amalgamation with the Old Comrade's Association in 1922, a recreation and reading room was built by public subscription at a cost of £1,500 in remembrance of Pershore men who served in the First World War. The club held a licence for the sale of beer, wines and spirits and also sold tea, coffee and soft drinks. It also contained a billiard hall holding three tables with ample seating for spectators, while the recreation room, in addition to being furnished with comfortable armchairs and tables, contained a fourth billiard table 'suitable for beginners'. Specified card games of skill were permitted, with draughts, ring quoits and chess being provided. The well-lit reading and writing room was of ample proportions with a number of daily and weekly papers available. There were billiard and snooker handicap competitions, fishing contests, quoits and cribbage competitions and a Slate Club, which at Christmas 1927 paid out over £200.

On 8 December, the club was visited by Tom Newman, known as the 'Billiard Wizard', who gave two exhibitions in the billiard room (*above*).

In 1977, a block of fifty-seven flats in Newlands was built by the Royal British Legion Housing Association and let to retired ex-servicemen and their families. The building was completed in May and opened with an impressive ceremony in the presence of the Lord Lieutenant of Hereford and Worcester in October of the same year. It was named Roland Rutter Court after an active member of the Legion who, after three years as Chairman, had died on a church parade. The ceremony was attended by civic leaders, the band of the 1st Battalion Mercian Volunteers with their mascot, and the standards of about forty Legion branches from across the county.

Spectators watch the opening ceremony. Among these were Mrs Rutter and her daughter.

A fête held at Avonbank by the Primrose League in July 1909. The Primrose League, an organisation for spreading Conservative principles, was associated with Lord Beaconsfield, whose favourite flower was the primrose. Formed in 1884, it became extremely popular and flourished in Pershore for many years.

The Pershore Ladies' Hockey Club, November 1910. In 1937, the Captain was W. Skinner with Vice-Captain M. Coates. They met at the Bottoms, their colours being a green tunic with a white top.

Above and below: A memorial service was held in 1910 to celebrate the life of King Edward VII, in which a great many members of various organisations took part. These two photographs show the parade turning into the High Street from Church Road. Firemen at the front of the parade in the first photograph (*above*) can be seen halfway down in the second (*below*). Known personnel are, firemen: C. Field (Captain), E. Nutting, C. Wright (Engineer). G. Daniels, Ernest Smith, William ?, ? Oswald and A. Wright, H Williams, J. Gould, Peter Hanson, S.W. Smith. Scouts: T. Willis, J. Grundy, Bert Cosnett, Sonny Howes, Leonard Twigg, Jack Mason, Percy Wilks, A. Carter, Jack Hemming, W. Dufty, A. and G. Bozzard, F. and E. Dolphin, B. Annis, Revd Hawkes-Field (Scoutmaster) and his wife. Ancient Order of Foresters: Herbert Bick (Secretary), John Vale, Fred Clarke, John Bick, Joseph Amphlett, T. Summerton, W. Pritchard, A. Morris, G. Champkin, John Edwin, John Langford, H. Perry. Postmen: Charlie Dolphin, Frank Goidfrey, Herbert Dufty, John Bell, George Bozzard, Arthur Hall, Arthur Mayo, Fred Bick.

A performance by Miss Pemberton's school, taken at the rear of the National School.

Opposite below: A plan of Pershore Racecourse, which was sited, until 1935, on Weir Meadow between Defford Road and the river. The course was said to be left-handed, over good pastureland and very easy to jump. The first recorded meeting is believed to have been on 26 October 1847 when the race was run in four heats of one-and-a-half miles when the bay mare, Amazement, owned by Mr Woods, beat Augustus and Perrot owned by Messrs Minor and Kirby. Later, two Hunt fixtures were held each year, in spring and autumn, the latter ceasing in 1929. Eventually flooding problems meant a move to a site near the High School, with the new course opening in October 1935. Being so near the railway station meant race-goers from places as far away as Birmingham and Gloucester could more easily arrive at the course, all of whom appreciated the new stands and other buildings. The last race meeting was held on 1 May 1939 as the Second World War had broken out before the autumn race was able to take place. During the war the course was commandeered by the military and used as an RAF training school, and the land, owned by the Earl of Coventry, was sold, later to become the site of the trading estate, its past history remembered in the name Racecourse Road.

Band of Hope, May 1913. There was an active group of the Temperance Society who were devoted to pointing out the evils of strong drink, meeting in the main at the Baptist church at this time.

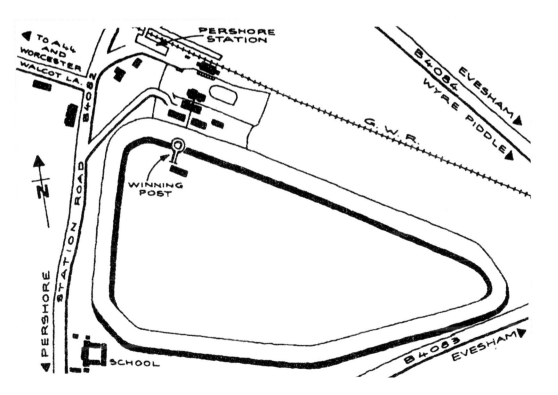

For some years it has been a tradition for the Croome Hunt to gather in Broad Street on Boxing Day. Earlier, it had met at The Star on the morning following the Hunt Ball. This photograph shows a meet in Broad Street on a rainy day in 1914. The once-flourishing hunt took on its present form in 1899 when the Hon. H.T. Coventry and G.D. Smith purchased hounds and re-founded the group. By 1910 there were fifty pairs of hounds under Lord Charles Bentinck, the Master.

On 25 May 1957, Princess Margaret attended a Girl Guide rally at Hindlip, Worcester, calling at Pershore en route where she was greeted by civic dignitaries. The photograph shows Mr Trapp, the Town Clerk, being presented to the Princess, watched by Mr Parkes.

five

Work and Play

At the beginning of the 1890s, a horse and cart carried a supply of fresh water to householders (at a charge of 1d a week per house) since the general supply was not up to standard, the majority of folk relying on wells. In 1902 reports on water supplies by Pershore Rural District Council stated that of a sample of forty-seven wells, forty-two were unfit and only five fit for domestic use, while in many streets the majority of houses were without water at all. The situation that year was further acerbated by a hot, dry summer.

This photograph has been lent by Mrs Mary Ricketts of New Zealand and shows her father's uncle, Frank (wearing the straw boater), who died in 1931. A series of large elm trees in Endon Hall Park, Wick, were chopped down and sold to John Hickman & Sons of Wolverhampton, usually being transported by horse-power, or, as in this case, steam engine.

Above: For many centuries there was a mill situated by the bridges, as mentioned in the Domesday Book, when Pershore was under monastic control. In 1840 a business was established by Mr Goodwin, the main cargoes being grain, building materials and coal, returning downstream with timber, stone, straw and flour carried by some twenty barges a month. This was succeeded by G. Partridge & Sons, who were still grinding flour until the mill was destroyed by fire on 15 July 1976. Another building was erected and continued manufacturing animal foods until it was sold recently and a complex of attractive riverside dwellings erected.

Right: Mr and Mrs George Partridge by the sluice gates. These gates were later updated, before being replaced on the side of the river by the Lower Avon Navigation Authority.

A fruit and vegetable market was held on this site until April 1910 when new premises were opened in Defford Road. It was another favourite spot for photographers so there are a variety of differing views of this event. The four 'P's on the hampers (which were made locally, in the main by M.J. Spiers who had workshops next to the river at No. 31 Bridge Street) stood for 'Pershore Produce Properly Packed', which cynical locals quickly changed to 'Pershore People Poorly Paid'!

The market in 1911. At the far end of Broad Street stands Myrtle Cottage (reputed to have had the first flush toilet in the town) with, on its left, the Victorian frontage of the Baptist church.

In 1959, the market in Defford Road celebrated its Golden Jubilee. By then cold-storage facilities had been introduced and pre-packaged goods were produced. The photograph shows produce in one of the bays at the market awaiting sale and distribution. In its heyday some 400 growers in the area would deliver produce to the Co-Operative Fruit Market.

Mr J.G. Payne, salesman, inspecting cauliflowers.

The construction of the Redlands flats brought into prominence the gasometers situated at the top of the cul-de-sac. Although it took some time for gas to become established in the town, by the late 1880s the Pershore Gas Co. had been formed. Mr William Smith, the last of the lamplighters, became a pipe-layer and gas fitter. By 1931 the company was known as the Pershore and District Gas and Lighting Co. under its chairman Mr E.G. Grizzell, with a registered office at Glengarth, in Station Road. The company went into liquidation in 1934 when it was taken over by the Cheltenham and District Gas Co. and was nationalised in 1947.

These unsightly gasometers sited at the top of Redlands were partly dismantled when this photograph was taken in December 1984 and finally removed in 1986.

In 1938, a Morris Commercial (registration CAB992) fire pump was delivered to the Pershore Fire Service at their station in Bridge Road, replacing an earlier Wolseley. Here we see Ben Hitchcock the Fire Chief (at back), Bill Lane (second in command), Vic Pugh, Mr Hirons, Mr Boulter, Mr Brant, Archie Fagg, Gilbert Surman (driver), Bob Lane, Sam Ball. During the Second World War the brigade was mobilised to fight wherever needed, serving during the Bristol bombings, at Birmingham and Coventry and even the London Docks.

Pershore's original fire engine, a Shand Mason steam-driven engine purchased partly by public subscription, was delivered to the brigade in 1900 under the leadership of Lieutenant Field. Years later this old engine was discovered lying in Mr Harrison's scrap yard at Lowesmoor in Worcester.

Above: During the Second World War the Fire Service was divided into thirty-two regions and became known as the National Fire Service. Captain Ben Hitchcock served throughout the war years and retired in the 1950s, by which time the group had become part of the Worcester City and County Fire Brigade. The photograph shows them on their move to the new fire station in Defford Road in the early 1960s when they took over the old drill hall, which they share with the Ambulance Service. From left to right: (1) Gerald Eastham, Chief Fire Officer of Worcestershire; (2) Divisional Officer Baker; (3) Sub-Officer Bob Holyoake BEM; (4) Col Harrison, Chairman Pershore RDC; (5) Alan Taylor, (6) Roger Smith, (7) Bob Southall, (8) Les Brooks, (9) 'Charlie' Dadge, (10) Ken Rimmel, (11) 'Kelly' Brant.

Left: Members of the Pershore Brigade during a 1960s Flag Day collection in aid of the Fire Brigade's Benevolent Fund. From left to right are: Ken Rimmel (wearing the newly introduced tunic), Alan Taylor, Brian Dobbins and Charlie Dadge (all wearing the older style).

Pershore Police Sub-Division, *c.* 1905. At this time the area covered by Pershore included Evesham and extended as far as Blockley, Gloucestershire, with officers in the old Worcestershire police often being transferred to the villages from Birmingham. From left to right, back row: Richard Jones (Blockley), H.J. Eales (Defford), H.L. Rose (Eckington), J.T. Norman (Hampton), F. Hill, (Elmley Castle), D.W. Turley, (South Littleton), J.A. Banner, (Evesham), H. Gummery, (Greenhill), W. Holder, (Bishampton), E.G. Griffin, (Bretforton), G.H. Evans, (Cropthorne), W. Arminshaw, (Evesham). Middle row: R. Underwood, (Pinvin), G.V. Phillips, (Broadway), H. Merrett, (Bengeworth), H.E. Harford, (Drakes Broughton), W. Howells, (Pershore), T. Hancock, (Harvington), J.G. Robinson, (Evesham), G. Davis, (Evesham), J.R. Thomas, (Bredon), R. Dainty, (Evesham), G.E. Johnson, (Fladbury), F.H. Taylor, (Pershore). Front row: A. Jones, (Evesham), W. Wagstaffe, (Bockley), -?-, -?-, -?-, F.H. Drew, (Broadway), -?-.

Prior to 1865, Pershore Police Station was situated in Bridge Street until a new station was built at the top of the High Street. In the 1930s the force again moved, this time to the corner of Worcester and Three Springs Roads. This new station included six police houses and also a courtroom where a County Court Judge was in session once a month and magistrates held Petty Sessions twice a month. When the Magistrate's Court was closed the buildings were sold for general housing and a new police station opened in 1999 in the grounds of the Civic Centre.

This photograph shows the force in the courtroom at Pershore Police Station, *c.* 1947. From left to right, back row: -?-, PC Cresswell, PC R. Farmloe, PC K. Emms, SC R. Phillips, SC C. Smith, PC F. Masters, SC W. Farr, PC F. Singleton, PC T. Dallow, SC. S. Mason, -?-, PC Taff Evans. Middle: PC F. Driver, SC N. Healey, PC J. Jones, -?-, SC Hicklin, SC C. Owen, SC R. Perks, SC W. Webb, SC J. Rowan, PC P. Savage, SC Carter. Front: PC E. Round, PC V. Davies, Sgt Lancelot, Supt Honeybourne, Capt. Stallard, JP, Insp. Lawson, PC B. Fuller, PC F. Andrews. [SC denotes Special Constable].

Opposite above: Abbey Garage, No. 79 High Street, was originally the Atlas Works founded by Edward and Thomas Humphries in the late 1840s. Here they began manufacturing engines, later moving to Station Road opposite the railway station when the original premises became a garage. The garage shared the site with the Central Market.

Opposite below: Abbey Garage in its early days when it was situated next to Pomona House which, in 1905, was the jam manufacturing works of Arthur Beynon.

Like most market towns, Pershore had something of a surfeit of butcher's shops. In the 1879 *Kelly's Directory* seven are named, including three in Broughton. By 1908 the number had risen to ten. Many of the butchers also owned abattoirs. One such butcher was in the High Street behind No. 64 (now apartments). It was opposite the old music hall, where in 1900, the butcher was William Wood. This photograph shows the hoist, which was still in situ when the building was converted in 1998.

This postcard, posted on 5 January 1906, shows the Atlas Works in Station Road, seen from the other side of the railway line. Moving to these new premises, which were on the site of disused brickworks, in 1883, the firm continued to prosper becoming internationally renowned for the reliability and efficiency of their threshing machines. They did not, however, forego smaller jobs – the town's lamp standards, of which, it is believed, only one now survives in a private garden, being produced by them.

Pershore railway station canopy was produced at Atlas Works when the factory was owned by Humphries & Co. in 1895. When this firm left in 1920 the premises changed hands and are now owned by Messrs W.H. Allen & Sons Ltd, who specialise in epicycle gearing. The building seen behind the canopy was at that time leased to Flowserve, later known as Val-tec, which reverted back to Allen's when Val-tec moved to Sussex.

Pershore station in 1920. Until 1852 rail passengers from Pershore needed to travel first to Defford, but in 1852 the Oxford, Worcester and Wolverhampton Railway came into being and a station was opened at Pershore in 1853. It is said that due to reservations regarding its inauguration by certain notables of the town, the station was opened in its present location, a good mile-and-a-half out of town.

In 1874, the down platform was extended, and ten years later a signal box erected. At the commencement of the First World War a temporary platform was installed in connection with army manoeuvres, and in 1927 a locomotive, the *Plymouth,* was renamed the *Pershore Plum* – believed to be the only train engine to be named after a fruit. This photograph shows locomotive 6965, the *Thorlestaine Hall,* arriving at Pershore in 1950, by then part of the Great Western Railway.

In 1934, a new halt was opened at Wyre, and, two years later, a new up loop installed at Pershore (this was reduced to a siding in 1965). The rail line at Pershore became increasingly well used and boasted a welcoming booking office and waiting room, and also attractive prize-winning platform gardens cared for by stationmaster Henry Jakeway. This photograph, taken in January 1964, shows a local bus waiting outside the station.

In 1957, a train travelling to Evesham suffered a derailment between Pershore and Wyre. Two years later another accident occurred on the 4.45 p.m. from Evesham back to Pershore. This engine, which was carrying a group of children from Prince Henry's School, hit a lorry carrying a load of lettuces at an uncontrolled level crossing near Charlton. Fortunately, none of the children were hurt, although sadly the driver of the lorry died.

Plum-spraying at Deakin's Fruit Farm. The egg plum came to be used as the basis for most jams due to its high pectin content, and was grown extensively in the area both commercially and domestically. August bank holiday seemed to be the day when the majority of people would harvest their crop, and having kept enough for their own needs would take the surplus to market. In times of glut these were piled on the ground, sometimes attaining a height above the surrounding sheds.

Above: Mr Deakin entertains his workforce at The Hall in September 1910. At times, between 200 and 300 people would be employed in connection with the fruit harvest and its processing, with whole families often taking part. As a rule, children were not employed, but any produce picked by them would count towards their mother's total.

Right: A group of plum pickers pose for a photograph sometime in the 1920s.

Opposite below: Cartons of egg plums awaiting transport. Hundreds of tons of fruit and other produce were despatched to all parts of the country, as far away as South Wales, the north of England and even Scotland, with produce arriving promptly the day after it was packed.

Until 1968, there were extensive hop fields at Wick Grange which was then owned by Mr Malcom Meikle. Hops were grown in ridges, with a crown that stayed in the ground and the top sliced off each year to encourage new shoots. These climbed up strings renewed annually by means of a large ball of string carried through a pipe at the end of a long stick, twisted onto hooks on the ground then to overhead wirework, the method of stringing varying between Kent and the West Midlands. Earlier, hops were grown up poles. The photograph shows stringing taking place at Wick Grange.

Each year, between 150 and 200 pickers would be hired from around Cradley Heath and Brierley Hill, having been hired by an agent for 1s and joined by a few local people and some gypsies. Rail fares were paid – two carriages being diverted from Worcester to Pershore from where the workers walked to the farm – and their luggage was also collected. They were housed in huts or sometimes freshly whitewashed cowsheds and given a weekly measure of potatoes and paraffin. It was routine for the workers to strike on their second day, prior to the fixing of wages which depended on the size of the crop and the ease of picking. Here we see the last load of hops to leave Wick in 1968.

The Poor Law Act of 1834 obliged the sick and aged to enter a workhouse in order to receive relief. This was generally an unattractive place, although Pershore seems to have fared better than most, since it was assisted by various charities. Such a building was opened in Station Road in 1836 at a cost of £3,000, controlled by a board of forty-three Guardians elected by ratepayers. A chapel was built in 1871 and two years later a detached infirmary; and by 1934 there were 220 inmates.

Pershore cemetery as it appeared in the early 1900s. The cemetery opened in 1875 and was for many years in the custodianship of father and son Edwin (1870-1957) and Cyril Smith (1905-92) who lovingly cared for the graves of the deceased. Cyril joined his father at the age of eighteen, and worked there for some forty-seven years. An additional area was added in 1950, being consecrated on 15 July when choir and congregation assembled. Unfortunately bad weather curtailed some of the ceremonies arranged by Mr Smith.

There have been several active football clubs in the town, including the Pershore Landrovers, seen here at Head Street in 1921. This was the year when, under the Chairmanship of Chris Cotterall, they won the Old Comrades Cup for the second year running. From left to right, back row: George Redding, 'Double' Long, Mr Mann, 'Packey' Rose, Chris Cotterall, Jim Cosnett, Jack Holder, 'Drummer' Baldwin, Vic Barber, Bill Young, Jim Summers, 'Laddie' Ballinger, Chris Annis, Jack Rock, Mrs Howes, Alf Teague, Chris and Grace Manton. Sitting and kneeling: Dick and Snowy Cosnett, George Teague, Bill Russell, Vernon Adams, George Haines, Tom Hewlett, 'Baggy' Grinell, 'Nippy' Rose, 'Sailor' Hirons, 'Langley' Coombe, Ted Middleton.

Above: Granny Clarke passing down Newlands when it was still cobbled. She regularly passed this way bringing produce to the market from Home Farm, Besford.

Right: Mr Arthur Smith is mentioned in the 1896 *Kelly's Directory* as being a chemist in the High Street. Said by the locals as being 'every bit as good as a doctor' he issued a regular advertising newssheet in which he also recounted anecdotes relating to the shop. He appears to have been a very enterprising man for at a torchlight procession celebrating the end of the Boer War he exhibited views of the fighting on a large sheet in Broad Street.

Opposite below: Pershore Rovers Football Club, who won the North Cotswold League during the 1913/14 season. From left to right, standing: A.H. Annis, W. Checketts, W. Lock, L. Hook, C. Edwards, T. Denning, A. Cambrey. Sitting, middle: W. Ballinger, G. Collins, A. Young. Sitting, front: B. Morris, L. Twigg, G. Young, S.O. Annis, C. Turvey

Sister Bolt was Matron of the Cottage Hospital in 1905. This was opened in Defford Road in January 1893, thanks mainly to Mr Charles Ganderton who left £500 for the purpose, providing an equal sum was raised. Fundraising was encouraged by Florence Nightingale and a hospital built at a cost of £1,141. Opened by Lady Coventry on 14 November 1895, by 1905 it had eight beds and a cot under the care of Sister Bolt, with four honorary surgeons.

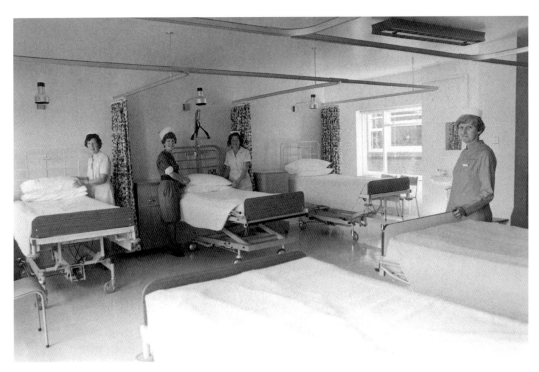

Pershore Hospital has flourished over the years, thanks mainly to the Friends of the Cottage Hospital Association. On 11 September 1976 a new ward was opened at the hospital.

The back of the old smithy at No. 102 High Street, which appears to be made up of three small cottages. Although the exact dates are not known, today's house is of Tudor origin with evidence of wattle and daub and a wealth of old beams. The first deed refers to a sale on 13 September 1704, and following a series of changes of ownership eventually passed to George Checketts who is named in the 1851 census as being a blacksmith at the site. By 1896 Harry Nash was residing at the premises, his son, James Gambion Nash, taking over the business where he remained until 1950.

The smithy itself was erected towards the end of the nineteenth century and was situated at the bottom of the garden. The name 'H. Nash' can be faintly seen between the windows behind which was housed the anvil and two furnaces and the door to the area where horses were shod. On hot days the necessary equipment would be brought outside, as on the occasion when this photograph was taken. It is not known who the men with James Nash are.

In 1932, the Friends of Pershore Abbey was formed by many prominent local citizens. Special services marked the first festival (one of which was broadcast) together with an outdoor procession of robed clergy through the town, and John Masefield, the then Poet Laureate, read some of his poems. By 1937 there were thirty-two vice-presidents, Col A.H. Hudson being the Chairman. These included many nationally influential people such as the Dean of Westminster, the Lord Bishop of Chichester and W.A. Cadbury in addition to well-known locals. At their fifth annual festival held on 2 July 1936 there was a 3 p.m. service after which tea was provided at the Angel Hotel. There then followed an address by Canon Hannay which, we are told, was 'full of humour but far too short'. It was reported that during the year the carillon had been repaired through the fundraising efforts of the Women's Institute. The bells had been turned and re-hung and the south transept cleared, with new vestries being dedicated on 16 April. This organisation has continued to flourish with annual summer festivals being held. George A. Birmingham was the preacher at the 1936 Friends Service held on St Peter's Day, 1936.

Above: The landlord of the Miller's Arms, Dave Henshaw, changes places with Mr Hussell, a customer, in August 1978. Mr Henshaw lost the top part of the second finger on his right hand in early IRA troubles. When he had a new sign painted for his public house he portrayed himself looking very much as in this photograph. This sign now hangs in the Pershore Heritage Centre.

Right: From 1699 until 1752, a well-known clockmaker was Pershore's Thomas Steight. Several of his clocks can still be seen in various parts of the country, this one having recently been restored in St James' church, Longborough, Gloucestershire. The clock is of the Turret type and has no dial, only a mechanism for striking the hour. This would have been mounted in a tower, driven by falling weights, wound up daily by hand. These weights drive the wheels and with a pendulum controlling the time and gear wheels with ratchets controlling the number of times a hammer hits a bell each hour. A century later another local man, Samuel Ricketts, was making grandfather clocks.

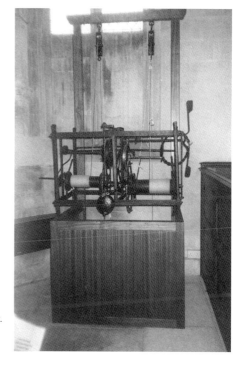

Above: Pershore Choral Society began life as a WI choir under the conductorship of Miss Joan Phillips (seated centre). By April 1949, when this photograph was taken, the group had been joined by male singers and the name changed to the WI Mixed Choir. This organisation flourished greatly over the ensuing years and now has a large membership comprising members from the town and surrounding villages.

Left: The Coles family of Coventry Terrace, Pinvin, celebrated their sixtieth wedding anniversary on 20 August 1947. Born in Ledbury, Mr Coles moved to Pinvin when he was four, his father being a signalman at the GWR station. Having begun his working life as a gardener at The Hall, he then worked as a mechanic in the moulding department at Atlas Works. Mrs Coles was the eldest of fourteen children. Her father, Mr Edwin Allard, was a shoemaker who carried out his business at his home in Fern Cottage, Pinvin. The Allards also celebrated a long marriage, receiving a letter from the King and Queen on their sixty-fifth anniversary.

Right: Revd William Walters first came to the town as a curate between 1857 and 1860, returning in 1873 as vicar and staying until 1894. During his time here he was chaplain to the Pershore Union for fifteen years, and Rural Dean for twenty-one years.

Below: Pershore Male Voice Choir. Left to right, back: G. Collins, F.D. Bott, H. Marshall, E. Nicklin, G. Payne. Middle: G. Bramford (accompanist), A. Rowan, A. Roberts, D. Trigg, E. Winkett, L. Broistow, C. Coombe, W. Russell, F. Main (deputy conductor), L. Brookes, J. Palfrey, F. Summerton. Front: W. Shelton, G. Hough, W. Sumner (conductor).

Above: In October 1973, Pershore Crown post office was downgraded to a sub-post office. This photograph shows the sorting office with, from left to right: Tony Lawrence, David Edwards (sub-post master), Bert Mills and Ray Summers.

Left: Perhaps the most internationally known of Pershore's past residents is Dame Barbara Cartland, writer of romantic novels, who later became an authority and advocate for healthy foods. Dame Cartland moved to Amerie Court in Newlands as a young child following her grandfather's financial crisis, and living there until 1917. As a young lady she was thoroughly involved in the 'mad, gay' times of the 1920s writing her first successful novel *Jigsaw* in 1925 and publishing 723 books by the time of her death in May 2000.

six

Best Days of
Your Life?

During the nineteenth century there were several academies in the town, both for boys and girls, some taking boarders, which children of the more affluent families attended. One of these was Dr Bushell's Academy (situated in Preston House) and also Mr Vallencourt's Academy where children were taught history, science and Latin, in addition to the three 'Rs'. When Dr Bushell's Academy closed, the school was taken over by Roy McCanan, an Irishman who originally accepted Irish boys only before moving to Besford Court. Children from poorer families went to dame schools, usually run by elderly women at their residences, parents paying a few pence weekly, the schooling being variable! Well remembered as one of the best is Miss Brickell's School for Girls in Bridge Street, and her husband's Boys' Academy in High Street, pupils paying 6d a week. Following the Education Act of 1870, the National School was built in Defford Road with free schooling for all. In 1853 a separate school for infants was built alongside until in September 1906 a new infants' school was built on a site in New Road, older students still being taught at the National School. After the County Senior School was opened, the National School continued as a junior mixed school. In 1937 it accommodated 230 pupils, before moving to a new site near the infants' school in 1942.

The boys' class at the National School, 1930. Boys and girls were strictly segregated, the classrooms and playgrounds separated by the house of the Master and Mistress who taught each sex separately.

Opposite above: Pershore Infants' School, 1920. Due to the National School being upgraded and enlarged, at the end of the 1880s the infants were, for a while, housed in three different places; the old music hall (High Street), the gymnasium (Worcester Road) and the Mission Hall (Head Street.) until the new infants' school was opened.

Opposite below: Apart from Eric Spalding (the boy standing on the left) the author has been unable to identify the children shown here at Pershore Infants' School in 1939.

In the 1930s, the top two classes at the school were divided by a green curtain, which called for a great deal of concentration from both students and staff. For warmth, Mrs Hallam's class had an open fire at one end and Mr Bramford's an iron stove at the other end.

Few of the pupils at the Junior Mixed School, seen here around the late 1940s, can be identified. Those who can be named include Raymond Heeks, Brian Griffiths, the Hirons twins, Rosalyn Davies, Lionel Swinbourne, ? Simpkins and Vicky Smith.

Pupils at the new County Senior School in Station Road have their photograph taken to mark the occasion of its opening on 12 January 1932. Later known as the County Secondary School, and subsequently as the High School, it opened with places for 480 children aged eleven and over from the town and surrounding villages.

The school opened with 413 scholars under a staff with Miss Ismay as Headmistress and Mr Pardoe as Headmaster. Others were the Misses Chambers, Jeffries, Lee, Skinner and Kite, and Messrs Halford, Matthews, Pointer, Howell, Robinson and Jones. This photograph shows them in 1959 with Rodney Baldwin, Mr Howell, Bob Ashworth and Miss Jeffries among them.

The Worcestershire County Council's School Library Service calls on the driveway outside the Mixed Infants' and Junior School.

Staff of Abbey Park Junior School, 1964. From left to right, back row: R. Brighton, J. Gardner and E. Adams. Front row: Miss M. Revers, G.H. Bramford (Headmaster) and Miss J. Hyde. In 1976 Pershore began a three-tier educational system with infants attending the recently opened Cherry Orchard First School and the Abbey Park First School. Abbey Park Middle School took pupils from both, the premises being enlarged to accommodate the larger intake. The middle school opened in January 1976 under the headship of Mr David Ward.

Mrs Dally's class at Cherry Orchard First School in 1974. Back row: Colin Emblem, Ian Manse, Adrian Fleur, Kenny Albert, Vince Ball, Adrian Taylor, David Hyden, Chris Durkin, Stephen Badger. Second row: Kenny Gubbins, ? Sallis, –?–, Craig Edney, ? Newman, Ian Edney, Gregory Burge, –?–, –?–, Third row: –?–, Diane ?, Susan Hale, Juliet ?, Samantha Carter, Heather Burge, –?–, –?–, –?–. Front row: –?–, –?–, Garry Gubbins, David Freeman, David Hemmings, Ian Mance, David Cundall.

The netball team at Cherry Orchard First School in 1974 with Mrs Edwards. They are, from left to right: Wendy McCreedy, Christine Roberts, Susan Shepherd, Melanie Roberts, Christine Freeman, Claire Leng, Jeanie Lewis.

Until 1967, those members of the Catholic Church wishing their children to receive a Catholic education needed to send them to either St Mary's, Evesham, or the Convent school in Worcester. Increasingly the need was felt for a local school in Pershore. This resulted in a new primary building being erected next to the Church of the Holy Redeemer. Built by John Hall in the space of eight months at a cost of some £36,000, it was blessed, and officially opened by Archbishop Dwyer on 22 May 1968.

Above: Mrs Kettle with some of her pupils at the Ley School, which was founded by former governess Miss Young, with six pupils aged four to eleven. Her assistant for twenty-three years was Mrs Elizabeth Kettle, who taught the younger children. Both ladies retired in 1971.

Right: May Day celebrations at the Ley School, *c.* 1956. In the centre is Richard Beeching and on the right Carol Lloyd.

Opposite below: In July 1994 there was a school trip to York. From left to right, seated on wall: Margaret Tacy (teacher), Candice Kelly, Sarah Lavender, Carly Gale, Sophie Abbot, Laura Chapman, Michelle Fuller, Siobhon Storey, Helen Cross, Emily King, Alana Hughes. Boys: Phillip Allison, Robert Mather, Scott Hyde, Anthony Cracknel, Daniel Wright, Patrick Archinhold, together with teachers Anthony Cracknel and Patrick Archinhold.

Past Principals of Pershore Horticultural College. From left to right: David Hall, Richard Martyr and Bill Simpson.

Avonbank House was built by the Hudson family of Wick in 1816, later becoming the residence of the Marriotts. As part of the post-war drive to enable Britain to become more self-sufficient the building was purchased by Worcestershire County Council, and Pershore Institute of Horticulture formed there in 1951 as the only establishment of further education in the land devoted entirely to horticultural courses, under its first principal, Richard Martyr. He was succeeded by Bill Simpson who handed over to Dr David Hall in 1991. The reputation of the college grew steadily and students today come from across the world, while the range of subjects has expanded to include floristry, business management, garden design and information technology, among others. In 1997, the college merged with Worcester College of Agriculture to become Pershore and Hindlip College, later also merging with Holme Lacy College in Herefordshire. Now under the headship of Heather Barrett-Mold, it covers some eighteen acres and each year holds an open day when thousands of visitors take the opportunity to see what goes on, to seek help and to stock up on first-class plants for their gardens, but this can be done all year round through a shop on the premises.

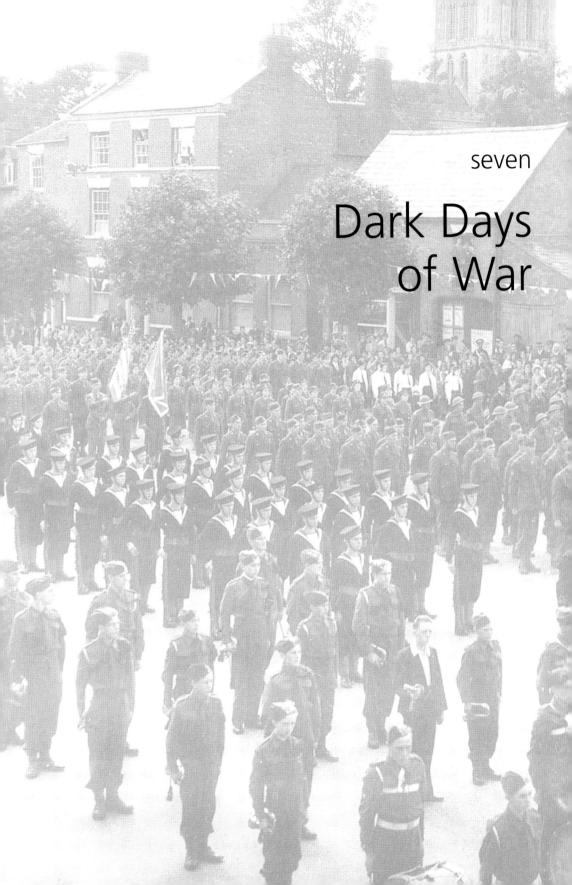

seven

Dark Days
of War

Officers and non-commissioned officers from 'F' Company, 2nd Volunteer Battalion, Worcestershire Regiment, in 1895. From left to right, back row: L/Cpl S. Cooke, L/Cpl J.G. Gardiner, Sgt B. Hall, Cpl T. Collins, Sgt C. Wright, Sgt S. Winwood, Cpl G. Collins. Second row: L/Cpl E. Nutting, Col.-Sgt J. Amplett, Lieut F. Checketts, Capt. E.T. Humphries, Sgt Inst J. Richie, Sgt S. Annis, Sgt R. Hook. Front row (seated): L/Cpl W. Winwood, L/Cpl F. Collins, Cpl S. Grinnell. In 1860 the country was not in a position to defend itself sufficiently so a volunteer army was set up – Worcestershire raising two battalions. Pershore recruited what was probably the largest company in the county, and became part of the second battalion.

Opposite above: No. 3 'D' Squadron Q OWH 1915 – the Pershore Troop. A report in the *Evesham Journal* states that several Pershore men were taken prisoner by the Turks on Easter Sunday 1916. Among the men were Sgt Sid Parkes, Arthur Blizzard and Dick Edwards.

Opposite below: Four members of Worcester Yeomanry, believed to be Sgt Frank Wood (is this the same man who was a member of the Pershore Hockey Club?), Sidney Faulkner and Sgt Allen. The fourth man is unknown.

Charles Thomas Milward, who lived in Broad Street, was a member of the Queen's Own Worcestershire Hussars, seen here at Kings Lynn, 1915. During the Second World War Mr Milward became a Special Constable, continuing to serve for some years. It will be noted that he carries his rifle by his left-hand side. This was the earlier method, which meant that if a rider was thrown, he was disarmed.

L/Cpl R.C. Edwards, known as Dick. This photograph shows the later method of carrying a rifle, with the butt on the left-hand side and sword on the right-hand side. A cheery letter, sent to Peter Hudson from R.C. Edwards when a prisoner of the Turks, was printed in the *Evesham Journal* of 29 December 1917 sending greetings from several of the Pershore Troop. Mr Edwards joined up on the day war was declared, having turned over his drapery business to Peter Hudson from whom he had purchased it and passing the military riding school examination on his first day.

The last Church Parade before sailing to the front, held at Kings Lynn, 10 March 1915. Among the soldiers in this picture are several Pershore men, including 'Tantine' Morris (on the left in the second row); next to him is 'Feather' Stone and Arthur Blizzard. Among this group are also Lewis (Dick) Hook (a sergeant in the Gallipoli campaign), Syd Faulkner, ? Shepherd, Charlie Milward, Sydney G. Parkes and D'Arcy Jones.

In June 1916, men of the Queen's Own Worcestershire Hussars and the Royal Gloucestershire Hussars became prisoners of the Turks following the battle of Katia on 23 April 1916, and were marched through Jerusalem to Ankara, about 500 miles away, travelling mainly on foot. At the front of the group are, from left to right, R. Blakeley, Sgt S.G. Parkes and Sgt Major Britain, with guards on either side of them.

A long line of decorated vehicles passes along a highly decorated Bridge Street, before turning into Broad Street by the Three Tuns Hotel. The parade is watched by hundreds celebrating the end of the First World War.

The Peace Parade at the end of the Second World War was a somewhat more sober affair than that held at the end of the First World War, although an impressive parade was still held. Contingents from many representatives of the armed forces gathered in Broad Street can be seen.

Above: In 1941, the golf course at Fladbury was taken over by the Ministry of Agriculture and a gun emplacement erected, before passing into the control of the Ministry of Works in 1943. The area then became a training centre for 3,000 American drivers. On their departure on 2 July 1944 the camp was used to house prisoners of war, both Italian and German. The photograph shows prisoners marching to the camp around 1946; most of them worked on the land.

Right: During the First World War women took over many of the jobs formerly undertaken by men who were away in the armed forces. Chief among their duties was land work and by the end of the war an embryonic Land Army Association had been formed. The photograph shows the uniform worn by these girls.

Mrs Marriott at Avonbank House invited girls from the Black Country for short holidays in exchange for helping on the land early on in the Second World War. They were treated as guests and invited to afternoon tea in the library, where they saw, although never met, blind men from Birmingham being cared for in the conservatory. The house later became a hostel for girls from the Women's Land Army.

The Women's Land Army was reborn under Lady Denham with, at first, little commitment from the Ministry of Agriculture. However, their worth was soon recognised for they undertook all types of jobs, from driving tractors and working in the dairy, to thatching roofs and even gassing rats. Here, girls staying at the hostel are seen with Mr Young, the father of Miss Young, the founder of the Ley School.

Another hostel, Hurstmead, was set up at Windmill Hill close to the railway line. A land girl's uniform consisted of fawn jodhpur-like trousers and socks, and a green pullover over a white shirt with an official tie. On their arm they wore a band bearing the initials WLA set under a crown surmounted by four diamonds.

Other hostels were established at South Littleton and Birlingham. For their day's work the girls were paid 11s and 10p from which they paid for their keep. With most girls from towns or cities they at first found their new regime extremely hard but soon settled into country life, many of them marrying and remaining in the area.

WINGS FOR VICTORY WEEK

Let's go!

The R.A.F. wants more and more aircraft. They can't do without them. In our "Wings for Victory" Week we can show by a record savings total

PUT EVERYTHING INTO IT —

3% Savings Bonds
1960-70

2½% National War Bonds
1951-9

Above: There was an active Army Cadet Company at the secondary school in 1941, many of the cadets choosing the Army as their preferred force when entering wartime duties. Among those seen here is Ken Perry (fifth from the left, back row) who later became a well-known and respected St John's Ambulance volunteer.

Plan of the airfield at Tilesford, 1943.

Opposite below: An advertisement for the RAF. In 1934 a field at Tilesford next to the racetrack was being used by Throckmorton Flying Club, operating two Tiger Moths which performed aerobatic displays and occasionally took paying customers for trips. During the Second World War this was taken over by the military and an operational airfield built for the RAF by George Wimpey and Co., the first personnel arriving in February 1941 under Flying Officer W.J.R. Warren before the huts and runways were finished. Eighteen days later Squadron Leader R.F.A. Williams took command, and so began RAF Pershore as No. 23 Operational Training Unit. There were also airfields at Defford and Wick, the latter known as Little Comberton. (The reason for this is said to be that the first radar equipment to be delivered, was sent in error to RAF Wick in Scotland, so the name was changed to prevent the same mistake from reccurring). There was also a WAAF camp at the northern end of Pinvin. Following the war, from 1948-52, the station became the home of the RAF Police Training School. In 1954 the main runway was lengthened and the airfield was taken over by the Radar Research Flying Unit from Defford.

On the afternoon of 19 May 1943, during a Wings for Victory Day held in Pershore, a Wellington bomber, one of several giving a flying exhibition, lost a wing and crashed into the roof of the Brandy Cask public house in Bridge Street, where it burst into flames. The crew of five were killed instantly. They were Canadians: Corporal Allam; and aircraftsmen Bande and Garvell; together with the pilot, Flying Officer Glyn Hynam, DFC, of the Canadian Air Force; and the Wireless Operator, Sergeant Peter Zoeller of the RAF both of whom were aged twenty-two. The two latter men were buried in Pershore cemetery with full military honours, their graves originally being marked by a wooden cross until these were later formally replaced by stone versions. In 2001, with the aid of the Heritage Centre, the Civic Society and the landlord of the Brandy Cask, a blue plaque was placed on the exterior of the building, commemorating the anniversary of the crash. This photograph shows the funeral of Peter Zoeller.

In 1940, a tradition was instigated by Pershore Youth Fellowship which had been formed in 1937. Having made collections through carol singing they purchased holly wreaths, laying them on the graves of servicemen on Christmas morning. This ceremony continued until the early 1970s when it was taken over by Pershore and District Royal British Legion, when the remembrance took the form of a poppy cross and was undertaken by various young people of the town including uniformed organisations. Each year, on the Sunday before Christmas, this poppy cross is laid on around eighty graves. Many of these are graves of airmen of the Royal Canadian Air Force, killed while flying from the wartime airfields. The sacrifice of these and of all the other young men from this area who died during the war is therefore perpetuated with thanksgiving and gratitude.

Other local titles published by Tempus

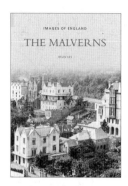

The Malverns

BRIAN ILES

This charming collection of over 200 archive photographs documents life in the Malverns from the 1860s until the 1950s. All aspects of everyday life are featured here, including shops and businesses, work and leisure and the war years. Local events such as the Bicycle Carnivals at Malvern Link are also recalled. *The Malverns* will delight those who want to know more about the history of the area.

0 7524 3667 8

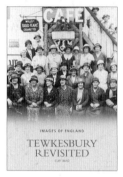

Tewkesbury Revisited

CLIFF BURD

This second selection of old photographs shows how Tewkesbury has developed from a vibrant trading post to one of the nation's favourite tourist places. With images of streets and businesses, as well as residents and visitors to the town, *Tewkesbury Revisited* will delight all those who have visited the area and wish to know more about its history, and will provide residents with a nostalgic look back into the past

0 7524 3476 4

Bromsgrove

ROBERT BARBER

The old market town of Bromsgrove, midway between Worcester and Birmingham, has long been a focal point for the surrounding villages and hamlets. This engaging collection of more than 200 photographs shows how Bromsgrove has changed over the last century. Local events are recalled, including the Assize of Bread, Ale and Leather conducted annually by the ancient Court Leet, and landmarks such as the Lickey Incline railway climb featured.

0 7524 1146 2

Motoring Around Hereford, Worcester & The Welsh Marches

A.B. DEMAUS

This richly illustrated volume on motoring in Hereford, Worcester and the Welsh Marches shows the many uses that wheeled transport has been put to. There are bicycles, cars of all shapes, sizes and ages, lorries, steam traction engines as well as views of motor sport in the area. Covered in detail are local manufacturers such as Morgan, now one of the largest independent motor manufacturers left in Britain.

0 7524 2361 4

If you are interested in purchasing other books published by Tempus, or in case you have difficulty finding any Tempus books in your local bookshop, you can also place orders directly through our website

www.tempus-publishing.com